Joyce Sutphen | *Modern Love & Other Myths*

Joyce Sutphen

MODERN LOVE
& Other Myths

Red Dragonfly Press

Text copyright © 2015 by Joyce Sutphen

ISBN 978-1-937693-68-8 paper
ISBN 978-1-937693-69-5 ebook

Library of Congress Control Number: 2015934594

Full acknowledgments printed at back of book

Cover painting: 'Endless' by Betsy Ruth Byers
(oil on canvas, 72" × 72", 2013)
www.betsyruthbyers.com

Typeset in Agmena Pro, a digital face created by Jovica Veljović

Printed in the United States of America
on 30% recycled stock
by BookMobile, a 100% wind powered company

Published by Red Dragonfly Press
Press-in-Residence at the Anderson Center
P. O. Box 406
Red Wing, MN 55066

For more information and additional titles visit our website
www.reddragonflypress.org

Contents

I

Start With This

So, by now you've picked the setting (someplace
by the sea — maybe a meadow at the
cliff's edge, a small white cottage in County Clare),

and you've put a human figure where there
was nothing since it was necessary
that something be awake and have motion

(though she could as well be made of marble
as flesh for all her stillness). Still you
stand her there looking out to the ocean,

thinking of the empty house she passed last
night deeper than the darkness all around,
and you realize now that she's been lost

ever since she left him, that a certain
kind of peace will never return (though perhaps
something better is on the horizon),

which is when you see the ship approaching,
coming full speed out of the sun, its sails
filled with golden sky, and you remember

a dream you had twenty or thirty years
ago about a boat flying over
the waters, but this time there's no singing,

just the overwhelming sense of wings (as
of Apollo), and you know what Leda
must have known, long before he let her drop.

The Seated Man

His back is to the ocean, with
the horizon on his shoulders.

Behind one ear, a cloud
rises. It is early morning

or evening. The remains
of his breakfast (or dinner)

are on the table, but he's
moved away to sit with

his back to the water,
in full sartorial elegance.

Two things glint: his glasses
and the pointed tips of his shoes.

His hands are clasped
and center him on the casual

throne he seems to have
assumed. "Approach," he says.

"Tell me the colors of the sky
and why you are here."

Whiteout

I have been, all morning, inside a book.
When I look up it is snowing — heavy
snow — and the wind is making a steady
run across the ridge of my neighbor's roof.

Everything is white-blurred, taken down
a shade, softened and yet forbidding, as
if warning that walking into snow is
different and more dangerous, as if

winter and cold had a hold on us
that summer never did. How quickly our
footprints disappear on a day like this,
and, after an hour or two, even a

body could be lost for months. I turn back
to the page where there was a fire burning.

On the Shortest Days

At almost four in the afternoon, the
wind picks up and sifts through the golden woods.

The tree trunks bronze and redden, branches
on fire in the heavy sky that flickers

with the disappearing sun. I wonder
what I owe the fading day, why I keep

my place at this dark desk by the window
measuring the force of the wind, gauging

how long a certain cloud will hold that pink
edge that even now has slipped into gray?

Quickly the lights are appearing, a lamp
in every window and nests of stars

on the rooftops. Ladders lean against the hills
and people climb, rung by rung, into the night.

Winter's Night

We are standing at the door after a party,
and a man I don't know very well says that

I should write a poem about the moon
and the winter's night, and now I wonder

what he had in mind — something about
a black branch against the white snow? —

or something about the way we all hesitated
to leave that house filled with wine and

flowers to linger in the cold — the cold,
which might be what he wanted me

to write about — the cold that cracks the house
at midnight and slices through the air

like a sword slipping into its sheath,
or the sound of ice-skaters on the lake,

their blades cutting slivers of the moon
into the dark surface of the winter's night.

Asleep in the Wheel

All year, when I jolt myself awake and
stumble into the shower, when my
sleep is a lean skin pinched between
midnight and dawn, I have no dreams.

I wake empty-headed, teeth clenched.
After months of this, I forget the word
for dog, so distracted by the blue sky
that my eyes deliver up pieces of yes and

no way to know at first that I am dreaming,
because they come like early snow, melting
as they touch the ground but after a while
one of them lifts me onto a train, and

I do not wake until the sun is a
small light in the roof of the drifted sky.

The Origin of Species

You call rare words into my mouth,
like birds to a feeder, one of them

appearing at breakfast as we ate our
croissants, and then later when I told

you about the teacher who ridiculed my
handwriting, you looked at me and said

that word, one of the endangered species,
one I thought was long extinct.

And now, what I think of is the moon
gliding in the sky under the eaves,

over the fringe of green horizon,
before the gathering of wings

and the first fall — and then of the world,
righting itself all over again.

You

You make me think in *italics*; you bring
exclamations to my lips! (I never
thought in parenthesis) — I always dashed
my way through everything! I

want to quote you; I want you to appear
in every footnote. I want you to be my
opening line. Yes — I have a lot of
questions; there seem to be some missing pages…

but I could live in an ellipsis; I
could become a demonstrative pronoun
(if you wanted that) or I could be a
questionnaire and you could fill in the blanks.

And now, although I'd like to say much more,
I must conclude — or what's a sonnet for?

Like That

I could not remember the beginning
line, which is almost as if to say I

could not remember my name — but that (too)
has happened, and I've survived. Memory

is like a sieve, a fringe made of fingers
trying to hold to the hem of the ocean —

the tide comes in, the tide goes out — green lung.
The thing I forgot was that we grow old

and find those "deep trenches" in "beauty's field,"
and I forgot because something else kept

coming to mind — a line about "nodding
by the fire," someone loving my "pilgrim soul."

Though everything else may slip away,
I won't forget I once was loved like that.

It's Amazing

Another word for that is astonishing
or astounding, remarkable or marvelous.

It's also slightly startling, which leads to
shocking and upsetting, perhaps a bit

disquieting, and that is troubling and
distressing — you could say outrageous

and deplorable, which leads to wicked
and more precise equations such as

sinful and immoral or just plain bad
and wrong. It's amazing, which is just to say

bewildering and unexpected, that
it happened out of the blue, and that we went

all the way from miraculous to absurd,
within the syllables of just one word.

Counting Sheep

This is not Crete, this is not
the island of Santorini; this is only
the shoreline of a dream I am leaving.

The sheep I counted had aspirations.
They distrusted gangways, wooden
chutes and the smell of gasoline.

For all I know, they might have been
wolves under all that fleece, fleet-
footed and capable of impersonation:

a shepherd, grandmother, faithful
friend. I swear I'll never count them
again, come what sleepless nights,

and what does it mean that I dreamt him
again, juggling the moon and the stars?

Combing the Shore

It seems obvious what should happen here —
almost nothing, or rather nothing with
a difference, if that suits you. Poets

and painters can make something out of
nothing and still be perfectly useless.
When I was a child I must have prayed for

a job like this, something close to dusting
the star on a church in the harbor or
watching clouds float over the distant hills.

Now, even though I begin to see how
desperate our situation is, how
deep and cold the water, I find myself

looking for the smoothest of black pebbles
to skip along the bottom of this line.

2

Goddess of the First Hour

As soon as there was time,
there was change.

If I did not remember you,
the sky would collapse;

everything I touch would fall
to pieces; even the stars

would leave their constellations;
the sky would be darker than night.

The world, as we know it,
requires an end —

a truth that has acquired
its beauty along the way.

The Fantasist

What is a man but his passions?
      — Robert Penn Warren, *Audubon*

If only it had been a real bird, neck outstretched, white against black,
    the wings beating a current through air.
If only he could have named it
    immediately.

He walks through the deep cold into the wind and sun.
Every morning before he begins work, he walks this road,
    noticing two things:
    the moon and everything else.

What was he doing before she turned in that wide room,
    windy clouds above the fields beyond the town?
What did he hear
    in the sound of her voice?

He leans in the doorway holding a cup of tea.
His hands have been shaping the shape of her again:
    her thighs, her feet, the back of her neck,
    all his creation.

He knows how to sustain her; the dream in the clay
    the way he'd lift and spin her
how he loved the moon that she was,
    how that was her name.

The Hampstead Sonnets
(The Real Thing)

That was the day I knew, although even
earlier — in Bristol, after we'd been
to Cornwall and back again — I could tell
something was happening to us, something
I wasn't expecting, something unplanned,
uncharted, and entirely amazing.
(I've looked up that word, "amazing," and put
it in another poem which explains
what happened much better than this will.) You
came down to London from The North because
I'd invited you, and even though I
never thought you'd come, you came, and I was
waiting when you rang the bell, and I was there
on Hampstead Heath watching the sun go down,
and then we went inside and fell in love.

We went inside and fell in love — easy
as I am telling it. Our shoulders touched
or didn't touch — it doesn't matter now —
but I could hardly breathe; I think I swooned
(when I'd never believed it possible);
I think my face went pale; I think my heart
was beating wildly — yes, I'm sure it was.
Next day we went to Richmond and to Kew
and walked through the palm house and the gardens,
admiring the gryphons and other beasts,
finding the pagoda disappointing,
the cactus houses overdone, but the
rhododendron grove was perfect: look at
the two of us, surrounded by flowers.

Later, the picture of the two of us
surrounded by all those flowers would go
into the fire with the other pictures
he found. Later, the letters that you wrote
would escape the fire and go for years
unread. Later — but what's the point? Later
is now, and now is too late to wonder what
we might have done with that amazing love
that came to us when we least expected
it, when we didn't know how rare it was,
when we — but I really most blame myself —
were afraid of saying the truth, afraid
the whole world would come down on its pillars,
afraid to hurt anyone else but us.

Anyone else but us might have made it
work; anyone else but me might have said
"Yes, wait," anyone else but you might have
asked again, but because of the distance,
because of the differences, because
of the dangers, the darkness, the dread nights
of the soul, I let all these things swallow
our words and then, for many years, silence
was all there was between us. Your letters
(and you'll never know how fiercely I fought
to keep them) went first to a friend's closet
and then, when I made the break I couldn't
make earlier, to my own apartment,
and then to my house where I live alone.

I live alone by choice and for pleasure,
and you have the life I had when we met.
I was a wife then; now you're a husband
and the father of daughters, just as you
hoped. Sometimes I remember us walking
on the beach in Cornwall, gathering slate,
"for pure and useless beauty" as you said,
and how we went later for tea and scones
and how later we slept on the cliff's edge
and (years later) I met you on a bridge
over the Thames just as I was thinking
of how once we had walked there together,
just as I wondered if that amazing
love we had was truly (yes) the real thing.

The Peaches

Back from the airport, I sat in the car
eating one of the peaches he'd given me.

It was a perfect peach, and the next one
was perfect too: two ripe, juicy, peaches

that I ate without regret. Even now
I can't forget the taste of that summer,

how I would open his letters as I
walked in a garden by the lake, reading

the words that were as close as words could come
to skin and the warm flesh that covered bone.

Then I thought of Properzia de' Rossi
carving the crucifixion in peach stone,

how she found the broken body of love
hidden in the tiny poisonous pit.

If This Be Error

You should come with warnings,
you should come with labels,
you should come with
directions that say

"Do not mistake this
for friendship, do not
combine with loneliness,
do not attempt this on your own."

You should come with instructions
written in large black letters,
every step numbered,
illustrated clearly.

It should say what will happen,
it should indicate what's next,
it should summarize
the situation.

There should be a way of knowing,
a way of telling what you're
thinking, there should be a
connection between

what you say and what
you do. There should be a sign
that says "High Voltage," "Do
Not Enter," "Thin Ice."

I should have been watching my step,
should have been more careful.
I blame myself for drifting with
the current, for believing

I could turn the tide,
pass through storms unshaken,
like the foolish moon or some
pathetic guiding star.

A Kind of Wild Justice

Living well is the best revenge,
and revenge is a kind
of wild justice.

I knew this when I stepped to
the edge, licking my fingers,
the delight of clouded

blackberries filling my mouth,
the little needle of regret
stitching out an ending.

Living well is the revenge
I will take I said
as I began

to walk on air, waving
an indifferent hand
at the stones

that wanted to nestle in my pockets,
at the long shadow waiting
for me to fall.

Riddled

What is heavier than my heart?
Don't pretend you know.

What is something you can hold
in your hand and never drop?

Tell me. Is there anything helpless
as speech when there's nothing to say?

What is a long time coming
and travels only in the dark?

What comes through the air
like a bird's song?

That's right. Don't pretend
you know that either.

The Perfected Presence

When you are with me now, everything
is in the right place, the way it never
was before.

We both say the right thing at the right time,
and when we are silent, we understand
what that means.

There isn't any need to make plans now
that everything happens as it should.
No surprise.

If this is paradise, is there no change
of death? Does ripe fruit never fall? (and so
on…and on).

For now, we wear their colors and play
their insipid lutes — this is not heaven.
You knew that.

Bent

Now I know — how can I describe this? — that
there are things I did not know were in me,

as when this morning I was looking for a piece
of paper, some small space of white to write

a list of what I hoped to do this day.
So filled (I thought) with serenity, I found

an envelope, unopened and addressed
to you, and just as I began to write,

something about your name (on the other
side) seemed wrong, and so I turned it over

to put a line across the name and crossed
and crossed it out and crossed it out again

and crossed and cried in anger and in pain:
the paper all in shreds, the pen tip bent.

Annunciation

Suppose the angel never comes.
Suppose you spend days waiting
in the empty room, staring at dust
in the ordinary beams of sunlight
falling from the high windows.

Suppose you scan the horizon and see
blue everywhere, suppose no one appears
in the doorway, no one descends in
a lightning flash saying the thing that
angels always say: "Fear not!"

and all of your hopes wilt on the stem,
the lily that was your emblem fades,
and you are not after all required
to bow your head to the impossible.

What then?

You leave the room. You marry
and have children who are not divine.
Your heart breaks in other ways.

Footnote

I would prefer to mention him only
in passing. How lovely to go back and

never to have met him, a connection
missed, a quiet night at home and no trip

to that city across the river where
he was waiting, but not (it turned out) for

me. I would prefer him as a footnote,
in parentheses, one small entry

in the index, the one that will baffle
the scholar who is reading carefully,

who realizes how impossible
it is for me to forget those lost years.

Always the Blank Page

He says, and I say always the bare tongue
and the clean cut of the horizon.

Who knows before she says it? Not I,
and even in the hum of consonant and vowel

I listen as carefully as any ear around me
knowing how much I do not see

and making up for the loss as quickly
as I can. He says, just get it down

on paper, just slip the wonder into
words, connecting faces at the table

to places on the globe, that little O
whereon we spin, and I say yes

(and yes again) — that's what I've
always done — earth, moon, setting sun.

Bird on a Wall in County Clare

Looks like a piebald rook,
a pinto crow. Portly, black-
stockinged, bright-eyed.

Walks along the flat slate
top-of-the-wall, head moving back
and forth on the rocker of his neck.

Stops, walks again, walks until
he reaches the last slate. Pauses,
glancing this way and then that.

Stands, steadies himself like a child
on the high dive. Gathers up his
strength and throws himself into the air.

3

Departure

One day you really do miss the airplane.
There you are, standing at the gate, and there
it is, climbing the sky without you,

getting smaller with every second.
You can't believe it at first. How could this
happen? How could they possibly leave, knowing

that you were stuck in traffic, knowing that
you were running down the concourse dodging
little clusters of people, who somehow

managed to be lifted up and down, out
of the sky, so that they could arrive on
time, the way you won't now, the way nothing

is ever going to be the same, since
the person you were supposed to love was
on that plane disappearing in the sky.

Mockingbird

A bird will usually repeat his song,
repeat his song, repeat, repeat, and I

was looking for a way to say how much
I am going to miss you, *already*

miss you, missed you even as I kissed you
good-bye. Good-bye, good-bye (I say good-bye!)

just like little Stevie Wonder did so
long ago and I wonder (wonder) who

(who), and right now is when the world goes on
spinning and the seasons come and go, and

it seems it will never end but it will
(it will). Look at us, how it only took

a minute to unmake all the loving,
leaving nothing there — just erase, erase.

The Last Straw

Some days you can lose just about
anything. Things can break in your
hands, rip loose in the wind, fall from
the shelf. They can go down the
drain, slip through a crack, roll off the

edge. And you? You just shrug your
shoulders, smile a wry little smile
and say, "Ah, c'est-ce la vie," or maybe,
"So it goes," or "That's the way the
cookie crumbles, baby." Other days,

spilling coffee on the counter makes
you weep; you see the toast crumbs
on the floor and curse your carelessness.
The whole world seems in pieces
because of leaves fallen from the

hibiscus plant, and when you see
that its red blossoms opened (at last!)
when you were gone and dropped like
ashes to the carpet — it's the
last straw; it just breaks your heart.

One Way In

This is how I hold my place in the world:
one line at a time, counting beats until
they come out right, chasing the sound of words
the way a dog chases cars to get her fill.

And this is how I fill my days: I slip
the ink across the page — a second skin —
and leave behind the color that my lips
print on the glass, a way of coming in.

This is how I stay in view: I take down
everything exactly how I see it,
I say it one way then turn it around
to see if there's another way it fits.

I hollow out a page to make a nest,
I stretch the pen out like a branch and rest.

Things to Watch While You Drive

The trees, slipping
across the fields, changing places with
barns and silos,

the hills, rolling over
on command, their bellies
green and leafy,

the sun-tiger, riding
on your rooftop, its shadow racing
up and down the ditches,

a flock of birds,
carrying the sky by the corners,
a giant sheet of blue,

the road, always
twisting towards or away from you —
both, at the same time.

Variation #25

This one is the darkest, she says.
After this variation, everything

is going up and up to heaven,
but for now, those two slurred notes

are the composer's way of expressing
grief, and grief is what we must

feel this July morning, distant jets
overhead, and a bird piping its one-

note song. What we never asked for
is what we want now, appalled at what
we have spent our lives gathering.

The Idea of Living

It has its attractions,
chiefly visual: all those

shapes and lines, hunks
of color and light (the way

the gold light falls across
the lawn in early summer,

the iridescent blue floating
on the lake at sunset),

and being alive seems
to be a necessity if you want

to sit in the sun or rub your
toes in the sand at the beach.

You need to be breathing
in order to eat paella and

drink sangria, and making love
is quite impossible without

a body, unless you are one
of those, given — like gold —
to spin in airy thinness forever.

Sleight of Hand

There are some things that I miss now, which is
why I can never describe what it was

that kept me from leaving long before I
did — a dream of happiness that moved like

a mirage across my heart and also
the shadow of obliteration that

fell from heaven like a giant bird
of prey but then turned into a dove, something

the magician pulled from a hat. It was
that simple, that mysterious. I stood

by, the volunteer from the audience,
ready to have silk scarves ripped from my throat,

and coins plucked from behind my ears. It was
when I found myself climbing into

the long coffin-shaped box that I wondered
how long even I would believe this trick.

Metamorphosis

If I could be anything to you,
I would be the rooftop, uncovered
by the flood, the stalk of corn,
standing after the hail.

I would be the crescent
reflected in the water bucket,
the woody taste of that liquid
in your mouth.

Then I would be myself in a
summer dress, barefoot on the porch,
the breeze lifting over grass
already drenched with dew.

We would lean
on railings
brushed white
by bristles of the moon.

The Lost Prophecy

What did you say about the moon?
Was it good? Was the moon a good
sign? Should we trust how it silvers
the hills and follow after it?

And what will happen to the fields
and the woods? Who will love
them when we are gone? And when
will that be? How long do we have?

And justice? Will there be justice?
How will it come, and will it be
mixed with mercy? Where will such
wisdom be found in all the earth?

Who will be watching then, who
listening? How will the things that are
coming be noticed by those who never
look up? The moon will be there.

What did you say about the moon?

One Thousand and One Nights

❦

After the first night,
it was easy. He had a taste
for plot, and it turned out
that I was good at suspension,
like the man who walked
a tightrope
between the towers —

I touched down
and never flew again,
but that's another one
of those stories.
Swans came into it
of course — the bell beat
of their wings and things
like that. My brother's hat,
my father in the city,
my mother scrubbing
floors, and my
sister (finally, my
sister) and then...

❦

I was sitting at my desk
when I heard a woman's cry,
but when I looked, I
saw that there was no one
there, and I realized
the cry must have come

from another time
and it was my own voice
I heard as I had heard it
speaking in another language
saying all the mysteries
at once, melting into
the most liquid of tongues.
I bent my head to read.
I cut the fabric into pieces
and put it back
together, differently.

Patterns,
it seems, are a way
of losing one's way
and also of coming home
again, but you can't
(I can't, we can't) go home
again — we've known that
from the beginning,
and so it would be a surprise
to find it (that is, home) has
been waiting for us all along.
The pages in his book
are empty. Another deception.
Somewhere it is all written
down in long scrolls —
or somewhere all the words are
burning, dissolving into
the wordless song of birds.

4

The Poem You Said You Wouldn't Write

The poem you said you wouldn't write
is the one that I find myself reading this

morning, and even though I should be doing
something else, I find I can't help writing

this poem about the sunlit patterns falling across
my desk, the sounds of cars starting up

in the neighborhood, and how it helps
to have these poems from you, the evidence

of things unseen, the substance of hope
that there will always be someone – the boy

sitting out on the front step with his transistor
radio, listening to news about Fidel Castro, or

the man sitting in his green lawn chair
watching how sky can be emptied of leaf,

branch, and trunk, until nothing is left
but stump and sawdust and your poem

about the tree, the one you said you wouldn't
write, the one that holds the branches high.

A Morning Poem

The first thing I see is
daisies brushed with mist.
The title is in a language I
cannot read, but I might call it
"Will It Rain Today?"

Next, the buildings: a red one
that seems to be a house, two
low barns, and something
white down in the distance.
There must be horses.

Beyond the fields are meadows
and the dark silhouette of trees
along the silver river's edge.
The water is wide and deep.
Who will cross it?

On the black brim of the horizon,
a cloudy sky is rolling a small
pearl of light into sun.
Who is already awake,
writing a morning poem?

Out There

The first time it was because
I'd never noticed it before;
the second was when I couldn't
remember that I had,
and after that it was simply
a matter of looking again.

I was moving even as I stood
at the window, watching the
swallows; I was content
even though I longed for more
than meadow, more than
April's green.

And sometimes it was because
of the wind, though it goes
where it wants and belongs
to no one, or it was for the way
the sun fell on the water
everywhere, because of the light.

And there were things we
seldom told each other because
we didn't know how to speak
such anger and such grief.
It was always out there,
but we never mentioned it.

The Hidden Word

Today, reading the last thing you wrote,
I think perhaps I have become your "you,"
though I don't suppose you'd admit it
just as I wouldn't presume to say

that you are mine. We use our eyes and what
we see is what we like to tell
each other, knowing how rare it is to
have eyes for useless beauty as we do.

You are one of those unexpected joys
as I am to you, time without its last
letter, a cryptic mention in a note,
but not what anyone else imagines:

a notable presence in the reading,
an absent pronoun only I will miss.

The One Constant Thing

We were talking about death
over the phone, speaking words into
a mouthpiece, listening to them
coming back into our ears.

I was looking out across the back yard,
taking in the curve of a tree
and the tall grasses dead in the swamp.
The light was early and golden.

You did not tell me, but I knew
that you could see — across the city
from sixty stories up — the lakes
and streets stretched out for miles.

I agree that whatever it is, it won't be
like this. I want to say I share your sense that
there will be someone there to meet us.
Yes, I suppose it's all we think about.

Two Reasons to Keep This Poem

Don't throw this poem away.
Keep this poem in your
pocket and read it when
(as is always your luck) you
find yourself in the slowest line
at the supermarket. Pull out this
poem, unfold it carefully, and
begin to read, your lips moving
ever so slightly. Soon everyone
in all ten checkout lines will
turn their lonely eyes on you
and a kind of hush will fall over
that fluorescent world as
they begin to shout: "The poem,
the poem! Read us the poem!"

Don't throw this poem away;
slip it into an empty notebook
and read to it every night and
listen to what it says in the morning.
Soon there will be more poems
than the notebook can hold:
some will fall in love and
get married; some will move
far away. After many years
the poems will have a family
reunion. They will sit down
and remember the way words
came together, how much they
liked the way things sounded,
and how they were surprised
as anyone by what they said.

Death Inc.

Without his scythe and crooked knife
he's simply an ordinary guy.

You see him at the bus stop,
and he's reading a folded newspaper,

or he's in the car next to you
on the freeway — first he passes

you, and then you pass him.
It goes on like that for a long time,

but though you glance over at him,
he never looks back at you,

which (it turns out) is a good thing.
All the while you've been

waiting for the carriage to stop
(kindly) at your door — the carriage

that would take you past the schoolyard
and the fields, accompanied by

the gentle clip-clop of horse's hooves,
but suddenly you realize he might be

driving an eighteen wheeler, high on
meth, tires screeching. Yes — it could

happen like that, but it's just
as likely he might be the shadow

of a tree you planted years ago
falling across the green lawn.

At the Cardiologist's

She thinks about things that have no meter,
things that cannot be measured in seconds,
things that have no heartbeat because her own
heart is broken now, and there is no cure.

He says that everything is looking
good: there are no blockages, no high risk
factors to consider; she won't die of
this for at least twenty more years — odds are.

If only she could sit in his office
all afternoon, watching little slices
of her heart beating so faithfully; if
only she can go on as steadily

as that, without even knowing what makes
it possible, without trying too hard.

Thinking With My Body

By touch I solve the problem,
fingertips and lips calculate
the difference.

Eyes are all surmisal,
unreliable; ears hear
what they want to hear,

feet touch, skins rub
together. Does it matter
whether or not

I stay the night? Being right
is cold and lonely
and only

the little gold watch, like
a company god, is paying
attention.

Even in My Time

Even in my time kingdoms fell,
and islands disappeared beneath the waves,
borders opened, and walls came down.
There were so many countries I would never see.

And even in my time, one tree died
and another one grew tall. The sky opened
and then closed, very slowly. Letters turned
yellow, and curtains faded in the window.

Friends who were once so dark and handsome
grew old. Bones in their spines crumbled,
or tumors filled the soft place under their
ribs. Sometimes their hearts stopped beating.

Even in my time, there were gardens filled
with flowers that would only last the day.

5

Transmigration

It will happen when the soul is ready
to leave the body at last. I suppose
there will be something in the way the light
falls, or the stars themselves will point the way.

Like birds we will gather as summer ends,
ready to mount the flyway our mothers
told us about long ago. We know there
will be a place for us when we arrive.

Whether or not this will happen again
is not clear. We often have the feeling
that we have been in these places before,
but for now it's only a matter of

waiting quietly for the wind to rise
and going along wherever it goes.

The Posthumous Journey of the Soul

What to bring along? Nothing.
Everything. Even the smallest rock
is too heavy to lift, and whether
you can carry even a bird's song
in your ear is uncertain.

And where to go? Not back along
those roads you knew when you
were living in the body — not even
into the dreams that came at night —
but somewhere out there, beyond
anything you have imagined.

There are some things you will recognize:
a palm tree beyond the last thought,
a thing with feathers that perches in the soul,
and a woman, lovely in her bones.
Once you pass the gate, it will be only
you…and the windy sky.

Two Things

Two things he loved — one for the way
it returned, and the other for the way
it opened — knowing neither one
would make it easier to relinquish
the idea of love.

When he looked to
the west, he could see her as a small
wing on the horizon, the one lit gold
for a minute when the sun slipped over
the horizon,

and she was there in the
flock of birds that twirled like a black cape
over the meadow,
and that was also her —
the humming return,
the last note in the box.

The Same Poem

You always write that one —
the one that's tattooed into
your bones at birth,

the one you hear in the wind
when you try to catch it, the one
you're always humming.

That poem is like another body —
lighter than skin and bones,
all heart and soul,

but you don't understand what
it wants you to say because
it speaks a language

you haven't yet learned
to translate. In the poem you
always write, you admit how

little you know and how grateful
you are for the worlds behind
the poem, the ones you

can only reach when you try
to write the poem —
the same one — again.

What the Clouds

All white and inside this room of moonlight —
my bones, my ashes, my small white headstone.

You point the camera and we are gone,
ages long ago, as in a storm. Keats

would have loved us and we him. Listen, you
hear the wind withdrawing…and then again,

and what I was hoping was that your luck
would change, that it would bring us together.

Perhaps some other life (there are others)
will let us stop when we pass each other

in the airport (this has happened before,
hasn't it?) instead of being swept on,

away — always away — from each other,
and there you stand, waving, as I ascend.

All the People I Used to Be

I was the kind of woman who brought
fresh bread and butter to class;
I tilted my head to hear your childhood —
just the sound of it as the trains passed
and the waves rolled onto the shore.

It was my intention to be with you
as long as you needed me, but you never
did (need me). I was the kind of woman
people don't mention, I was very ordinary —
except for that heart of mine when it loved.

I used to be able to keep still — one
hand held the needle as the thread passed through;
I filled the cup to the brim and carried
it across the room, and when I wrote that
last word, you could see each letter clearly.

For the Evening Light

If you listen carefully, you'll hear
at least five kinds of birdsong
threaded through the air.
It isn't necessary to name them.

That sound a minute ago was a train whistle.
Even though it is very quiet now
you must not forget that somewhere
a train is moving through the woods.

Practice this way of letting go:
put your fingers around a rose
and twist it off the stem. Scatter
the petals to the wind.

Tell yourself the truth about him
and then erase it. Go to the window
where the light has disappeared
behind the trees. Say good-bye.

At the End of Things

Before it gets to a confusion, there's
a moment when everything is still
deliberate — one word, holding on

to another, facing each other, placing
their palms together, saying: This much
we know; this much is true. After that they

wave, and one of them gets on (or off) the train —
it really doesn't matter which one, where he
goes or what she says. Love stops making sense

at least in the way they counted on, long
ago, and as soon as those words are out,
they are lost. She ends up on a curb

waiting for a ride that will never come,
and he's already forgotten her name.

Breathing

Once I made my mind up
it was easier. It was

simply a matter of doing what
I said I'd do, one step

at a time. The wind outside
was cold, just as it had been

before, but I put on my layers
and wrapped a scarf around

my throat. There were so
many more difficult things

we'd have to face — floods,
earthquakes, sickness, and

death. The small omissions
that happened in the course

of a day were (now that I
saw if differently) mere motes

in the afternoon sun, lovely
little pieces of dust.

No matter what was coming —
that wave, still far out at

sea — I wanted to go out and
breathe this hour's golden air.

Say It

Say that it is the continuous life
you desire, that one day might stretch into
the next without a seam, without seeming
to move one minute away from the past
or that in passing through whatever comes

you keep coming to the faces you love,
never leaving them entirely behind.

Say that it is simply a wish to waste
time forever, lingering with the friends
you've gathered together, a gradual
illumination traveling the spine,
eyes brimming with the moment that is now.

Say that it is the impulse of the soul
to endure forever. Say it again.

The Book of Hours

There was that one hour sometime
in the middle of the last century.
It was autumn, and I was in my father's
woods, building a house out of branches
and the leaves that were falling like
thousands of letters from the sky.

And there was that one in Central Park
in the middle of the seventies.
We were sitting on a blanket, listening
to Pete Seeger singing "This land is
your land, this land is my land," and
the Vietnam War was finally over.

I would definitely include an hour
spent in one of the galleries of the
Tate Britain, looking up at the
painting of King Cophetua and
the Beggar Maid, and, afterwards
the walk along the Thames, and

I would also include one of those
hours when I woke in the night and
couldn't get back to sleep thinking
about how nothing I thought was going
to happen happened the way I expected,
and things I never expected to happen did,

just like that hour today, when we saw
the dog running along the busy road

and we stopped and held on to her
until her owner came along and brought
her home — that was an hour well
spent. Yes, that was a keeper.

Acknowledgments

"Whiteout," *Water~Stone Review*.

"Start With This," *Water~Stone Review*.

"The Hampstead Sonnets," *Water~Stone Review*.

"Combing the Shore" in *Water~Stone Review*.

"Sleight of Hand," *The Gettysburg Review*.

"Mockingbird," *The Gettysburg Review*.

"The Poem You Said You Wouldn't Write," *The Gettysburg Review*.

"Death, Inc." mnartists.org: *What Light* Series.

"At the Cardiologists," mnartists.org: *What Light* Series

"Winter's Night," *Flurry*.

"Book of Hours," *The Writer's Almanac*.

"Even in My Time," *The Kean Review*.

"The Perfected Presence," *The Kean Review*.

"Say It" (published as "Say It Again") *The Kean Review*.

"Footnote," *Dogwood*.

"The Peaches," *Bareroot Review*.

"If This Be Error," *Margie, The American Journal of Poetry*.

"It's Amazing,"*Blue Earth Review*.

"A Bird on a Wall in County Clare," *Shenandoah*.

"The Idea of Living," *Knockout*.

"The Morning After," *Knockout*.

"The Seated Man," *Knockout*.

"Annunciation," *The Georgia State Review*.

"The Posthumous Journey of the Soul," *Great River Review*.

"What the Clouds," *Magma 36* (UK).

About the Author

Joyce Sutphen grew up on a farm near St. Joseph, Minnesota and currently lives in Chaska, Minnesota. She has degrees from the University of Minnesota, including a Ph.D. in Renaissance Drama.

Her first book, *Straight Out of View*, won the Barnard Women Poets Prize (Beacon Press, 1995, republished by Holy Cow! Press in 2001). *Coming Back to the Body* (Holy Cow! Press, 2000) was a finalist for a Minnesota Book Award, and *Naming the Stars* (Holy Cow! Press 2004), won a Minnesota Book Award in Poetry. In 2005, Red Dragonfly Press published *Fourteen Sonnets* in a letterpress edition, and 2010 they released *First Words*. *After Words* followed in 2013. Sutphen also co-edited an award-winning anthology entitled *To Sing Along the Way: Minnesota Women Poets from Territorial Days to the Present* (New Rivers Press, 2006).

Her poems have appeared in *Poetry*, *American Poetry Review*, *Atlanta Review*, *Minnesota Monthly*, *North Dakota Review*, and many other journals, and she has been a guest on *A Prairie Home Companion*, hosted by Garrison Keillor.